Sales Skills To Live By

Closing the Deal: Mastering Sales Skills in the Insurance Industry

By

Jay J.P. Peak

Copyright © 2023 by Jay J.P. Peak

All rights reserved. No part of this book may be used or reproduced by any means, graphic, electronic, or mechanical, including photocopying, recording, taping, or by any information storage retrieval system, without the written permission of the publisher except in the case of brief quotations embodied in critical articles and reviews.

Index

Introduction

Over the years of successful insurance sales, I have developed many ideas that have worked and failed. People look at my success and want to know what my big secret is. I will be the first to tell you that success is obtained through failure, and failure is my motivation to become successful.

The more people tell me that they don't need "any more insurance," the more they thank me for helping their family by "giving them peace of mind."

When you look at what an insurance agent does, you soon realize that it is hard to define. You might say that we help reduce risk or that we help protect families against catastrophic events. My belief is that "we help people." That's it! No long explanation or wording. If you approach every sale as an opportunity to help that person or family, I promise you will feel more fulfilled and make more sales. If that is done, your job becomes your career, and your career becomes your passion.

So how do we take your passion and turn that into dollars? It is my quest to help you make more money and waste less time. I will outline how to get prospects to call you! Make bigger sales! Have more time to enjoy life. Isn't that why you have big dreams and ambitions? If you think big, you will sell big. And big sales mean big money!

The main focus of my training will be to help insurance agents increase their sales by generating more targeted and qualified leads through tested marketing techniques, how to be more prepared before the sales meeting with the client, understanding personality types, sales motivation techniques, and developing centers of influence that will develop your book of business. Finally, I want to help you develop a superstar mindset and unleash your inner potential.

Please use these techniques and make them your own. My recommendation is to take a few things from this handout and focus your energy on perfecting them.

Getting Organized

Preparation is the key to your sales success. Most insurance agents that are new to the business use the shotgun approach. They don't know much about the business and are just trying to get their feet wet and make a living.

Unfortunately, this causes a lot of problems in the long run, such as agent retention, low sales numbers, low morale, and uncertainty in the future. This is why so few agents make it past the first two years in this field, and for some of those who do, it is always a struggle because they don't have a system that will generate leads.

If you will spend time studying your product and your market, put together your sales kits, and have some type of customer profile, you will be years ahead of the game.

Let's first talk about the product you are selling. If you don't understand what you are selling and how it will help or hurt someone, don't sell it! You must know the impact of how ABC products can change the way someone feels or has felt in the past, or you won't sell anything at all.

Your market demographics will vary. Some good ideas to look at are married people over 40, people that have kids in school, a social group or ethnic group, or members of a large club that share a common interest. The idea is to find out what you are looking for. The simple fact is this: if you don't know what you are looking for, how will you know when you find it?

Sales kits are for winners, and winners are prepared for their prospects. Be sure you have the right tool in your tool bag for the job. You should have applications, visual tools for the sale and stories about how it helped someone, and all of the proper documents to turn in the sale. Get this ready before you meet the client so you won't have to fumble around to find what you need.

Lastly, a customer profile should include a person that you would like to work with, such as someone interested in the same things you are. It should be a specific profile about them that will give them the ability to purchase from you. Mine is a family of more than two that owns a home or a business owner that makes a combined income of $100,000 and cares about his or her family.

I'm not saying you need to turn down business if your prospect doesn't match your profile. What I am saying is that if you look, you will find them. You can get referrals of potential clients from them working with your perfect client most of the time.

Goals

Before you can go anywhere, you need to know where you are going. A goal can be several things, such as having more family time, a better car, being the best at something, owning a home, or trying something new. It can be as simple as "I want to make more money." Whatever it is, if you focus your selling efforts on that one single goal, it will be a lot easier to hit. I think too many people try to spread themselves too thin. They try to get everything all at once. When they don't get it, they become discouraged and quit.

When you establish a goal, be sure to write it down and associate it with a picture and a thought. For example, if you want a Ferrari, cut out a picture of them from a magazine and put them where you can see them. Don't put them in just one place. Put one on your nightstand and tape one to your mirror. Put a picture in your office and look at it often.

Do you ever feel down about something? Or that you can't concentrate on what you're doing? Look at the picture and remember what you are working for.

Also, when you drive the car that you currently own, imagine that it is a red Ferrari. When you get in it, think about the leather and how it would smell. Turn on the engine and imagine that you just turned on a V-12 beast. Trust me, if you make a list of your goals, live and breathe them every day, and believe that you will have them, I promise it will come true. All you have to do is trust yourself.

Goal Tracking

Winners keep track of their sales so they know when they cross the finish line. Now that you have defined your major goal, break it down into smaller goals.

For example, if you want to make $100,000 per year, then break that down to $12,000 a month or $400 a day. That breaks down to $50 an hour if you work 8 hours per day. Ask yourself if you are worth $50 an hour. If you say yes, then you must start to think like you are.

Look at every situation that you put yourself in and ask yourself, "Am I making $50 an hour right now?" If the answer is no, then you're on the wrong track. The way a superstar thinks is, "I won't touch it or do it unless it makes me money." The point is, if the insurance policy you are selling makes you less than $50, and if you spend more than an hour with them, you need to find a different market or product to sell.

Also, it is a good idea to keep a dry-erase board with a calendar on it. As each day goes by, always remember to put how much you made for that day on the calendar. If you didn't make any money that day, put a big red X in that spot. If you made less than your goal, put a yellow X in it. Finally, if you made your goal, write the amount in green marker and add it to your monthly total.

This small and easy task will not only help you keep track of where you are, but it will also motivate you to see more green and less red. Remember, green equals money! Red equals poverty!

Scheduling

To double book or not to double book, that is the question! When you look at any professional's schedule, such as a dentist, doctor, or attorney, you need to remember one thing: customers are there because of their expertise. If you're worth seeing, they don't mind waiting or moving their appointment up an hour or so.

When you make your schedule consider these things: decide what time you want your appointments to begin and end and how much money you want to make. Decide how many appointments this will take and add 20%. In using the previous example of making $100,000 a year, we said that it breaks down to $400 a day. So how many appointments does it take to make $400 a day? 1, 2, 3, or maybe 5.

Let's say it takes three appointments to make $400 a day. We all know, based on Murphy's Law, that if something can go wrong, it will. I always add 20% to any number I try to achieve. So that means I need at least four appointments per day, just in case one cancels their appointment.

Out of the appointments that you set, you have four chances to make your $400 today. You could hit a home run and make it all in one. Or you could sell 3 or 4 smaller policies and make your goal as well. By working with the 20% rule, not only will you make your goal, but at the end of the day, you might just end up with more money!

The times that I would recommend to set your appointments are 9 am, 11 am, 1 pm, and 3 pm. The reason for this type of schedule is you can move someone an hour ahead if you double-book and both appointments confirm. It also gives you time to make your prospecting calls in the morning, from 8 am to 9 am. It also allows for a lunch break and time to do administrative work. If you have a good day, you may be able to cut out a little early to make more family or fun time.

Numbers Don't Lie

Earlier, we talked about goals and how to keep track of your numbers. If you start to associate what you're doing with a number, it will help you stay on track. I want you to have a millionaire mindset on every appointment, every day. Don't be afraid to ask for a bigger sale.

What's the difference to you if you ask for a $10 check or a $100 check? This seems to be a big mental block for a lot of agents. There are times when you feel like you can't afford what they are buying, so who are you to ask them? Take the approach that you are an educator, not a salesman. Based on their current needs, if the $100 option is better for them, tell them that and say it with confidence. Remember, you're there to educate them, not sell them.

You should know what your product costs and how it works. The client is more impressed if you can tell them a rider on a policy cost $5 more per month without having to look it up. You can say something like, "Your insurance premium will be $95 a month, and for $100 a month, you can add the disability rider, just in case you get hurt and can't work anymore. Doesn't that make sense?"

You just added an extra $5 a month, which is $60 a year. If you do that five times a month, it becomes $300 more in annual premium, and if you do it every month, it becomes $3,600 more premium a year. See what I mean about knowing your product?

Spend a little time to get to know how it works and be prepared. In this example, you made an extra $3600 in annual premium. Another way to think about it is you just gave yourself a $3600 raise by knowing your product. Not too bad, is it? Sometimes you don't need to sell more policies in a year. You just need to work smarter.

15 Second Commercial

The 15-second commercial is one of the biggest overlooked areas by agents. Any time you work for a company that sells something, they ask you to develop a couple of sentences that will capture another person's attention.

Careful care should be taken. You are asked every day what you do, and you need to have an answer. Remember, you are a salesman! How many times have you asked someone what they do, and you realize that if they ask you, all you can say is, "I sell insurance." People need a reason to continue to talk to you after you have met them. If they lose interest, you lose a potential prospect.

I am going to give you some suggestions on how to accomplish a great commercial. Once you create one, you need to memorize, memorize and memorize it. The subject of insurance can come up in several ways, and if you have it memorized, you can possibly develop a lead.

A 15-second commercial is not just something to say. It is your lifeline in the insurance business. And remember to listen for opportunities to tell people about you. They come up more often than you think.

Steps to Creating a Killer 15-Second Commercial

Get a paper and pencil for this. You will need to take notes and brainstorm ideas. Don't take this lightly. Spend some time on it, and you will be rewarded for your hard work.

1. Write down what you do. Not just "I sell insurance" or "I help people." Put some thought into it. If you start your commercial with a heart-felt reason why you help people, it will carry over into the message that you are trying to deliver. Also, think about the impact that your product has on people's lives. This will help you discover your inner potential and develop sincerity.

2. Make a list of the products that you sell and write down why you sell them. Don't write, "I sell them to make money!" Really do this; it will help you tremendously in the long run, especially when a customer asks you why they need the product you are trying to sell them. If you don't like a product, then don't sell it. Too many agents try to know, love and sell every product that their company sells. Focus on your favorites and offer what you believe in.

3. Write down what product or products you will focus on. This will help you with your business planning. It will help you listen for keywords and conversation topics to interject your commercial. You need to make your commercial interchangeable with the product that you want to talk

about. Such as, I help people with their (life insurance, health insurance, etc.)

4. Write down how you can help someone with a particular product, such as life insurance. Ask yourself, "Why does someone buy life insurance? What does it do for the insured, the beneficiary, and the family?"

5. Now write down three reasons why you would buy the product. If you can't come up with three or you don't like the product, don't sell it.

6. The last sentence of your commercial should ask the customer to meet with you, tell you if they have insurance, or start a conversation about their insurance needs. Put this last line in the form of a question.

7. Now that you have brainstormed all of the reasons and attributes of the policy you are trying to sell, start to organize it on the page. Make it into a paragraph form. Read it aloud.

Once you have a rough idea of what you want to say, share it with your mentors and people that will give you honest feedback. I will give an example on how this process works below. Remember to put this into your own thoughts and words. Don't rush through this process.

Brainstorming your 15-Second Commercial Example

What do I do? - I help (individuals, business owners, young families) provide for their families when they can't anymore.

Products That I Sell- Life Insurance, Health Insurance, Dental and Vision Insurance, Annuities, Long Term Care Insurance, and Cancer Insurance.

Product focus for this 15-second commercial will be - Life Insurance.

How Does Life Insurance Help People? - I believe I help widows in their greatest time of need. I help families stay in their own homes when a loved one dies. I make it possible for children to go to college if a parent passes away. I lessen the burden on a loved one. I help spouses with income when there is none. Finally, I provide a way for families to pay for final expenses.

Three reasons why I would buy Life Insurance - To keep my family financially secure if I die; this would be a love gift to help take care of my spouse and protect her dreams and finally lessen the burden that the loss of income would have on her.

15-Second Commercial Example

Example 1

I help families protect their well-being and assets by providing Life Insurance that would help keep them in their own homes and provide an income for their surviving spouse and children. Tell me about the planning you have done for your family.

Example 2

I work with business owners to help educate them on how to protect their business assets and employee retention by providing insurance products that are designed just for them. How many employees do you have?

Example 3

I work with company executives to provide customized insurance plans to meet the changing needs of high-income earners. Who customizes your plans?

Prospecting Ideas

The goal of prospecting is to find people who are interested in buying from you. It sounds pretty simple, but how do you find these people? What is the best way to convert them into sales? The ideas that I am going to share with you will help give you a baseline to start from. I would pick 1 or 2 of the ideas from the list and make a marketing plan for them. Include things like: what is it that you are going to do? What is the cost? How can I implement these strategies to make money for myself? How much time will it require? How much effort will it take to put the marketing in place? If you develop a plan in the beginning, you will have success at the end.

Marketing Events- Have a way to attract customers to your booth, such as give-a-way or free picture, blood pressure test, or an "enter to win" type strategy. This is a great way to have people come to you. I like to take party pictures at a lot of events. After I take the picture, I hand them a business card that has a web address on it. Once they go to the web address to see their picture, a capture page asks for their information. They can enter it if wanted or skip ahead and go to the main page. On the main page, the client can print, download, upload to Facebook, or share the picture with their friends. This is cheap to run and maintain and is easy to set up. All you need is a camera, a $150 website, and an event.

Walk And Talks- These are a good way to hand out your flyer! When you are entering a business, hand a flyer to them and give your 15-second commercial. You will also need to take one of their business cards for a follow-up call. Here is an example of what to say:

Agent - (Hand the person behind the counter your flyer) "Hi, my name is _________, and I am the agent in your area. I help local business people with their (Health Insurance, Life Insurance) insurance needs. Do you have a business card?"

Prospect - Here you go (they hand you the card. Be sure to verify that the name on the card is the person that you are talking to).

Agent - "Thank you so much for your time; I'll be in contact with you."

I would recommend that you do 15 Walk and Talks a day. They are easy to knock out when you are in between appointments. Make folders for your cards and separate them by day (Monday-Friday). Whatever cards you pick up today, put them in tomorrow's folder so you can call them. Now, here is a good opening commercial to get them to talk to you!

Agent - "Hi, this is _________ from ABC Insurance. I was the one that gave you a flyer yesterday. Did you have a chance to look at it?"

Prospect - "No, I threw it away."

Agent - "That's great! It was cleverly disguised as a junk piece of paper! What it was describing is how I help business owners with their (Health Insurance, Life Insurance). Is Tuesday or Thursday better for you to talk about yours? (From here, you will handle objections and set the appointment!)

Networking Events- I love networking events and think that this is a great way to make extra sales. Some agents focus on this one marketing idea and are very successful. The only thing that I would tell you is to make a goal for the number of business cards that you are going to collect and go to meet new people. Very often, we get too comfortable at these events and miss opportunities. It is very easy to talk to people you know or met last time. Don't fall into this trap.

Clubs and Organizations - If you have any kind of hobby or interest, there is probably a club for it. Examples include car clubs, Masons, Rotary, cigar clubs, boating and sailing clubs, hunting groups, military associations, and golfing groups. This type of networking is not quick, and it takes a while to develop relationships with the other members. Don't go into these types of things expecting quick sales. This is a good way to develop centers of influence and sell bigger cases.

Project 100 - Just about any insurance company that you work for will ask you to write down the names of people you know and to call on them to sell them insurance. I like this idea, but I think you need to be careful not to push sales on to your family. You can also get your feelings hurt if someone you are close to tells you no! I work my project 100 slowly as I see them from time to time. I use stories of how I have helped people to spark an interest in what I am selling. This is a soft approach, and it works great for me. If you do this with love and don't try to just sell them something, you can have a successful project 100.

Book of Business - Obviously, you need a book of business before you can call on them. This is a gold mine for future business. I do mailings, calls, and client appreciation days to drive more business. A lot of insurance agents try to focus all of their attention on getting new clients and neglect their current ones.

I would seriously consider putting this strategy into play as soon as you start to develop a book to work from. Remember, they already bought from you before, so you know they like and they trust you. Why wouldn't you use this to your advantage? Don't miss out on selling someone in your book of business another product. If they aren't buying it from you, someone else is selling it to them.

Golf Tournaments - During the summer months, you can sponsor a hole on the golf course during tournaments. This can also be an "Enter to Win Give-a-Way" such as a "Hole in One" or "Closest to the Hole" on a par 3. The expense of these events can range from $50 to $300, depending on the cost to sponsor the hole and the prize given away.

Enter to Win - You can incorporate an enter-to-win type of drawing into almost any event or club that you belong to. The basic idea is that you are "giving away something." All they have to do is put their name, address, phone number, and the insurance product that they may be interested in on a form. You will have a drawing on a certain date, and if they win, you will call them and give them the prize. I have devoted my time and effort to this campaign. I think it is one of the easiest and most profitable marketing campaigns for me. I combine this marketing technique with a lot of events that I do.

Referrals - During my appointments and networking, I developed Centers of Influence to send me referrals. This has always been an important part of my business. I never stop doing this. I have attorneys, funeral homes, friends, and family, and my clients refer business to me all of the time. This one idea nets me 30% of my business. Be sure to educate these people on what you do so that they can talk about you when something comes up.

Exploring 15 Diverse Lead Sources for Insurance Agents

Generating leads is a fundamental aspect of success for insurance agents. To build a thriving client base, agents must tap into a wide range of lead sources. In this chapter, we will explore 15 diverse lead sources that insurance agents can leverage to expand their customer reach and grow their business.

Referrals from Existing Clients

Referrals from satisfied clients are one of the most valuable and effective lead sources. Encourage your current clients to refer their friends, family, and colleagues to your services. Offer incentives or rewards to clients who provide referrals as a way to foster a positive referral culture.

Strategic Partnerships

Form partnerships with professionals in related industries, such as real estate agents, mortgage brokers, financial advisors, and accountants. Collaborate with them to cross-refer clients, creating a mutually beneficial relationship that expands both businesses' networks.

Networking Events

Attend industry-specific networking events, conferences, and community gatherings. Engage with potential clients and other professionals, and exchange contact information for follow-up discussions.

Online Lead Generation

Create an engaging website and optimize it for search engines to attract organic traffic. Utilize online advertising, social media markcting, and content marketing to generate leads from internet-savvy audiences.

Social Media Platforms

Leverage the power of social media to engage with potential clients. Share valuable content, host webinars, and participate in industry-related discussions to build your online presence and attract leads.

Purchased Leads

Consider purchasing leads from reputable lead generation companies. However, exercise caution and thoroughly vet the sources to ensure the leads are of high quality and match your target audience.

Cold Calling

While cold calling requires persistence and resilience, it can yield promising results when done correctly. Research your target market and approach potential clients with personalized offers tailored to their needs.

Direct Mail Campaigns

Send targeted direct mail campaigns to potential clients in your local area. Personalize the content to address their specific insurance needs and include a compelling call to action.

Seminars and Workshops

Host educational seminars and workshops on insurance-related topics. Position yourself as an industry expert and use these events to generate leads from engaged participants.

Community Involvement

Participate in community events, sponsor local organizations, and support charitable causes. This involvement can create positive brand recognition and lead to referrals from community members.

Online Reviews and Testimonials

Encourage satisfied clients to leave reviews and testimonials on your website or review platforms. Positive feedback can enhance your credibility and attract potential clients.

Professional Associations

Join relevant professional associations and actively participate in their events and discussions. Networking with like-minded professionals can lead to valuable referrals.

Lead Magnets

Offer valuable lead magnets, such as free e-books, guides, or checklists, on your website in exchange for visitors' contact information. These downloadable resources can help nurture leads into clients.

Customer Surveys

Conduct customer satisfaction surveys and collect feedback from existing clients. Use the insights gained to improve your services and identify potential opportunities for upselling or cross-selling.

Other Specialist Referrals

Encourage your team members to refer potential clients from their personal networks. Offering incentives for specialist referrals can motivate them to actively participate in lead generation.

By tapping into these 15 diverse lead sources, insurance agents can build a robust and steady stream of potential clients. Each lead source comes with its unique advantages and requires tailored strategies to maximize its effectiveness. Diversifying lead generation approaches will not only help agents reach a broader audience but also enable them to adapt to changing market dynamics and remain successful in the competitive insurance industry.

Marketing Tools

Signs - You can make your own or have them screen printed. The sign should have what you are selling on it, a catchphrase, and, most importantly, your phone number. If you do this consistently and over time. Your phone will ring off of the hook, so be sure to answer it!

Flyers - Focus on a flyer that has only one product on it, not a list of everything that you sell, so that it is less confusing for the prospect. Make sure you have your name and phone number on it.

Fish Bowl Meal Drawing - This is a weekly drawing for people that put a business card into a Fish Bowl. Draw one card from the bowl each week and invite them to eat a free lunch with you. Also, have them invite 5 of their friends to come as well. This way, you can target more people at a time. A pizza place is a good place to do these. The prospects can get a buffet and drink for around $8.00 each. This campaign will cost around $40.00 a week and $160.00 a month per location. If you do this right, you should have no problem getting business out of this idea.

Luggage Business Card Tag - This can be used in conjunction with the Fish Bowl Drawing. The observant person may be saying, "What happens to the business cards that you collect and don't call?" The answer is that every card collected can be made into a luggage tag and mailed with a letter to the prospect. Follow up after you send the letter. The luggage tag becomes a great conversation starter. Be sure to put in the letter where the drawing was held and that the luggage tag is a second prize!

Qualified List of Prospects - This is a good way to get to the prospects that you would like to cold call or mail something to. What you do is find a list-selling company like Sales Guinee. Give them your demographic information, such as age, income, zip code, and any other profile-building information that you would like your list to reflect. And they will compile all of this information. And come up with a list of names for you to call on or mail to. Most of the time, they will even scrub the list against the Do Not Call List as well for you.

Predictive Dialers - A predictive what? A predictive dialer makes cold calls suck less. In this day and age, there is a real concern with sales professionals in regard to the Do Not Call List or the "DNC." And if you call someone that is on this list, you could have big fines. So when a go-getter decides to call out of the phone book, he is handcuffed by the system. Out of all the people in the phone book, the majority of them are on this DNC list.

Also, you don't know who you are calling and if they are even the type of customer that you are looking for. So what you do is purchase a qualified list of prospects that meet your criteria and load them into your predictive dialer. This is usually a web-based system that is controlled by a 3rd-party administrator. And let the dialer do all of the hard work for you.

Depending on what kind of dialer you get, it will dial 1 to 5 lines at a time. This speeds up the process of waiting on someone to answer the phone and also the time it takes to manually dialing the phone.

And when someone picks up the line, the dialer will pause the calling, and you are connected to your prospect. You then give your

15-second commercial. This is a great asset if you have telemarketers in your office. It keeps them on the phone and talking to people.

Lead Capture Website - In the information age that we live in, it is important to have a web presence. This can be achieved through a Lead Capture Website. The basic idea is you set up a page that tells about you and what you do. Then as people go to the website, then they enter their information in the "Request More Information" section. Once this is done, you will get an email with all of your contact information. Finally, you call the prospect and set the appointment.

These websites cost only $100 to $150 to set up. And you can put your website info on any advertising that you do. You will be surprised how many people feel more comfortable entering their information on a website than calling you directly.

SEO - SEO stands for "Search Engine Optimization." This is how you get your website ranked on Google or any other search engine website. The basic idea is you find an expert in SEO. Then they look at your website and optimize it for the search engines. Then they make sure it shows up on the first page of the search engine when you type in a keyword or phrase.

This type of advertising can be expensive. But it is also very effective. You should consider this if you want to generate your own leads instead of buying them.

Direct Mail - The numbers on your return on investment on direct mail is about half a percent to three percent. However, if you can do this cheap enough, you should be able to make a nice profit off of a mailing campaign. I would stress to you that it is better to do smaller mailings to a targeted group than a large shotgun blast.

This is mostly true because it is better to do several mailings to the same list than one big mailing and only send them something one time.

Seminars - A seminar is a great way to get in front of a lot of people at the same time. You generally put out some kind of newspaper ad, TV commercial, radio ad, or direct mail to generate traffic to the seminar location.

I would caution you on doing too many of these types of events in a short period of time, mostly because they take a lot of time to set up. The biggest problem that you will run into is getting people to come to the seminar. If you can master this, you will have a great way to generate sales.

So what's the secret to having a successful seminar? Here are the basics. First, focus your message.

For example: Don't miss out on an opportunity to retire tax-free! Local Expert Joe Agent will be conducting an Educational Workshop on Tuesday, March 19th, where Joe will explain advanced retirement techniques that the IRS does not want you to know about.

Here's what happened in that message. We had a hook "Retire Tax-Free!" We told them that it was an "Educational Workshop," not a "Sales Seminar," and told them why they needed to come. "Learn what the IRS does not want you to know."

Second, attract the prospects with food or prizes. This will make the difference between a .25% response on your advertising to a .75% to 1% response on your advertising.

Third, Stick with it! You are going to have good, bad, and ugly seminars. This is a known fact! And you need to be prepared to do several seminars to be successful.

And for those advanced techniques? Here are my recommendations. First, Mail and Radio have worked best for me. I'm not saying that the others don't work. But in my experience, those media have had the best results in my area.

Second, you should only do your seminars on Tuesday and Thursday nights, not weekends, holidays, or church nights. I would also encourage you to offer two nights in a row. Join us on Tuesday and Thursday Nights.

Third, you need to have a lot of advertising volume. My best results are when I mail out 5,000 pieces per seminar. So if you do a Tuesday and Thursday night, that would be a 10,000-piece mailer. I know this sounds like a lot, but that's what it takes to do an effective seminar.

Finally, have a budget. My typical budget per week of seminars (2 a week) is $8,000 to $10,000. You will need to keep this in mind if you are starting out.

Prepare for the Sale

If you are prepared before you walk into a sale, it is a lot easier to sell. If you do a couple of small things before you meet them, it will help you tremendously when you are closing the sale. Here are a couple of things that I do to make my job easier:

1. Make a folder with the client's name on it with these items in it:

   a. Print the quote for the product you are trying to sell. Also, print variations of this product just in case the client wants more or less insurance than you originally talked about.

   b. Put the application and any other forms that you might need for the sale (HIPPA authorization, replacement form).

   c. Have a summary sheet in the folder that has all of the information on it that you have collected so far. (Name, address, phone number, social security number, kids' names, and spouse's name).

   d. Lastly, make sure you have anything else you may need, such as (an underwriting guide, paper for notes, and a pen)

Powerful Sales Techniques and Phrases

I'm going to list some great techniques that really helped me with my sales. You should find someone to roll play with you and help you sharpen your mind.

The Take Away - If someone is unsure about a buying decision, take it away! For instance, if someone isn't sure about their decision in a life insurance sale, tell them about the underwriting process and that we will have to see if they can qualify. A lot of people think they are superman, and this is a shot at their ego. This is a great way to sell type A people.

This is what I Would do - Give them your honest opinion and advise them what you would do for their family. Remember that you are the expert. And if they trust you, they will go with your recommendation.

In My Professional Opinion - If you are recommending a specific type of policy, lead into the close with, "In my professional opinion." This sets the stage for you and builds your credibility.

Doesn't that just make sense? - If you want to see if a client is on the same page that you are in the sales process or they aren't responding well to your questions, ask their opinion! This will also help them open up to you.

With That in Mind - This is a great transition phrase that is easy to use, especially after you just overcame an objection the client gave to you. "With that in mind, is this going to be a business check or a personal check?"

Do You See the Value? - Another great check question. If you want to see if the prospect is on the same page you are.

What Would You Do? - This question helps get the prospect in the right mindset. Simply ask one of the spouses what they would do if the other one died.

Bang Your Dead! - If you are talking to a couple, ask what they would do if the other spouse was dead right now. This helps establish uncertainty in the prospects' minds about the future.

Tell Me How This Can Help/Hurt Your Family? - Let the prospect tell you why they want to buy insurance. I think this will surprise you. A lot of clients will talk themselves into buying the policy. All you have to do is write it up.

The Cheaper Option - Prospects know that you work off of commission and that you want to sell them something. So sometimes, if you feel like there is a trust barrier, recommend the cheaper option to them. This helps establish that you are not trying to just sell them something.

Pick the Middle One - An old technique for sales is to give the prospect three options, a low, medium, and high option. Most of the time, the person will pick the middle option. This is a psychological advantage for the salesman. The prospect doesn't want to be cheap, and they don't want to get ripped, so the middle option is an easy out for them.

Your Custom Plan - As an insurance agent, it is your job to recommend the best option for the client. Use this to your advantage. As you are coming up with options and adding riders to the policy, tell them what you are doing. This is also a great line to put into your 15-second commercial. "I will customize a solution for your needs."

Explain The Process - This is a great closing technique. People are afraid of the unknown. If you explain the process of applying for insurance, you can remove uncertainty. Also, you can use this as an assumptive close, "Mr. Prospect, what will happen is that we apply for coverage with an application, along with the first month's premium attached. We will go through the underwriting process and check your medical background. After this is all said and done, we will come back with an offer. At this time, you can accept or decline the policy. Now with that in mind, what's your social security number?"

Tell me what you understand - I use this phrase when I am about to close the sale. For Example: Mr. Jones, tell me what you understand about what we just went over.

This is a great way to make sure that your prospect is following along with you. Also, when they repeat back to you what you just went over. Mentally, they lock in the sale. Because they now understand the reason that they are buying your product.

Hot Buttons

A hot button is the reason someone is meeting with you. Hot buttons are also associated with a feeling like love, pain, or uncertainty. If you can find the real reason someone is buying, the sale becomes a lot easier. The easiest way to find the hot button is to ask probing questions like, "Why are we meeting today?" "How do you feel about that?" "What kind of impact did that have on you?"

This takes some practice, but if you are good at it, you will definitely increase your sales. You should role-play with another agent and ask as many questions as you can think of. This will help develop your skills.

Personality Types

This is a skill that you will learn over time. If you have a basic understanding of personality types, you can then understand why someone is motivated to buy. Study the four types of personalities below and start paying attention to customer behavior, such as whether they are talkative or shy, very detailed in their questions, or offer just basic information.

Once you get a good grasp on their main personality type, look a little deeper. Most people are not just one type. It is very common to find a combination of two or more characteristics. The first personality type refers to how they interact with other people in daily activities. The second is usually a backup personality or is under the surface. For example, someone may have an outgoing personality, defined as Sanguine. They may also be good at paperwork, having a Melancholy backup personality type.

To really understand other people's personalities, you must first understand your own. I would recommend finding a book about this subject and taking a self-administered personality test.

- *Sanguine-* Life of The Party, Optimistic, Extroverted, compassionate, and thoughtful.

- *Phlegmatic-* Laid Back Personality, Easy Going, Very Receptive and Shy, Often Prefers Stability to Uncertainty and Change.

- *Melancholy-* Very Analytical, Bean Counters, Perfectionists (Accountants)

- *Choleric-* Type A Person, Hard Driving; They Like To Be Leaders and In Charge Of Everything.

Buying Motives

Most people don't buy insurance because they woke up this morning thinking it was a good idea, even though they may tell you that! Their buying motives are usually associated with pain, a catastrophic event that happened in their life, or someone they know.

If you can find this motive, you have found the reason you are sitting down with them to sell them something. You should ask probing questions to find out what this motive is. Based on what you find out, you can usually attach a dollar amount to it.

For example, you may discover that the person that you are meeting just had a friend pass away in an automobile accident. This motivates them to think about their family, especially their spouse. They are thinking about, "What if it happened to me?"

You should ask them hard questions about this subject. Remember you are the expert, and you need to be in charge of the conversation and lead them to the buying decision.

Some questions that you can ask are, "How did this affect their family?" "What do you have in place to protect your loved ones?" When you start to understand their motive, you uncover the pain. Now you have every opportunity to sell a policy. You can use phrases such as, "John, if something was to happen to you tomorrow, a $500,000 policy is only $250 a month. In my professional opinion, this would help ease the pain if something was to happen to you like it did your friend. Wouldn't you agree that this is a good buying decision for your peace of mind?"

Wow, now we are getting somewhere. If you approach every meeting like this, you will sell so much life insurance that you can't keep your phone from ringing!

Listen to What They Are Not Telling You

There are a lot of reasons that a person buys something and a few reasons they don't. Let's focus on why someone might not buy. This will help you understand how to close them and ask for the check.

The biggest reason someone might not buy from you is that they don't trust you. From the very beginning, you need to establish trust by being sincere and caring about their problem. Let them know you are a real person, not just a salesman. Finally, make every sale personal to the customer and treat them like you would your own mother.

Another reason someone might not buy from you is money. There are many things to learn about sales, but you cannot help a broke customer. Unfortunately, you will run across people that want to meet with you and don't have any money. I'm not saying that you need to treat them any differently, but you do need to spend your time wisely. When you run across this, help them where you can and move on.

The last reason that we will talk about is time. Time is one of the most precious commodities that you can have. Time allows us to make better decisions and not be so stressed out all of the time. Often enough, you will run across someone who just won't meet with you and cancel appointments over and over again. This will kill your business if you're not careful. I always set an appointment, send them a letter to confirm the appointment, and call them the day before and the day of the appointment. This eliminates excuses not to meet with me.

I will be the first to tell you that things come up and your schedule changes. But, if this happens repeatedly, more than twice per customer, move on to the next person. I know insurance agents that will chase a lead until the cows come home. While they are chasing a one-appointment dream, I'm selling to people who want to buy today and making it a reality.

Work Smart, Not Hard

Killers to any insurance agent's day are things that waste time. We're going to talk about what they are and how to avoid them. Also, I will discuss how to optimize your day to make it profitable for you.

First, what is a time waster? A time waster is a distraction, person, poor planning, technology, or personal endeavor that makes you less money and takes away from your focus.

A couple of popular ones for insurance agents are reading your email every 30 minutes. You should set aside a time of your day to do this activity. I read mine in the morning before I start my day, about 7:45 am, and then <u>once</u> before I go to bed.

Going on one-legged appointments will also hurt you. A one-legged appointment happens when your prospect is married, and the couple can't meet together, or one refuses to meet with you. Don't waste your time and try to reschedule the meeting. If one of the spouses refuses to meet, then turn and run. No matter how promising it looks, very few couples make decisions without each other.

You should also line up your day where you have specific times that you do things, such as reading your email in the morning before you start your day. Have specific times that you can meet clients. This will greatly help you in your scheduling.

Hire An Agency Assistant

You can be a great insurance agent and sell a lot of policies. But if you can't follow through with the client. You won't be in business for very long. This is a common problem for agents that are hunters rather than gatherers. A hunter will kill its prey, and it's pretty much over for them. All of the excitement has gone away, and there is nothing left for them to do.

A gatherer will collect all of the information needed and is only satisfied after the long winter has passed, and he still has food left. This, to him, is a success. The kill is just the means to supply him.

So where am I going with all of this? Well, first things first, most insurance agents are hunters, not gatherers. And this can be a weakness that needs to be addressed early on. It's ok to only be a hunter if you have someone following behind you to pick up the pieces along the way.

So an agency assistant will help the hunters through those long winters. Or, in your case, they will help keep your cases on track, keep the cases current with any requirements needed by the underwriters, and do all of the paperwork that you hate.

Depending on your state, you should also consider getting them licensed to also sell insurance. This way, the assistant can sell policies over the phone if the opportunity arises. Also, a lot of states require an assistant to be licensed if they have anything to do with the case. So it's just a good idea to go ahead and spend the time to do this

The cost of hiring an assistant will be well worth it. I believe in the long run, this is one of the best ways to put money into your agency, and it gives you a good return. Just imagine if all you had to do was hunt, and all of the rest was taken care of for you. Just in customer service alone, you will have happier customers and keep more clients.

Superstars Don't Cry

The first and most important thing you can do is to remove all of your mental blocks. Positive thinking is the key to your success. If you get into stinkin' thinkin' and are around negative people, it doesn't matter what you do today, tomorrow, or next week. Your results will always be negative.

Did you ever wonder why someone can fail at something and someone with a positive attitude can do the same thing and make a ton of money? This is proven every day in the insurance business and in your personal life. Next time you're out and about, start paying attention to people who like their job and the ones who hate it. I promise that their attitude directly affects their work life, family life, and their business life. Don't fall into this mind trap.

Whatever type of product that you're selling, be sure you believe in it. Know that it will help the customer in a great way. Don't let your mind be trapped into thinking that it is not a good product or that you feel like it's priced too high.

Remember that all of your customers believe in you. They trust that you believe, understand, and back your product 100%. The sale is just the end result. Be positive and stay positive. It will take you places you only dreamed about.

Cultivating a Winning Mindset for Success in the Insurance Business

Entering the insurance industry can be both challenging and rewarding. To thrive in this dynamic field, a winning mindset is crucial. A winning mindset empowers insurance professionals to overcome obstacles, seize opportunities, and achieve unparalleled success. In this chapter, we will explore the key components of a winning mindset and how to apply them effectively in the insurance business.

A growth mindset is the foundation of a winning attitude. Instead of viewing talents and abilities as fixed traits, individuals with a growth mindset believe that their skills can be developed and improved over time through dedication and effort. In the insurance business, embracing a growth mindset allows you to continuously learn from experiences, seek feedback, and adapt to changing market conditions. Embrace challenges as opportunities to learn and grow, and see failures as valuable stepping stones towards success.

Setting clear, specific, and achievable goals is essential to building a winning mindset. Define your vision for success in the insurance industry and break it down into smaller, manageable objectives. Visualize yourself achieving these goals regularly, as this mental rehearsal can enhance motivation and focus. When faced with challenges, draw inspiration from your vision of success to stay committed and resilient.

Maintaining a positive attitude is a powerful tool in the insurance business. Positivity not only boosts your own confidence but also attracts clients and colleagues. Cultivate optimism by reframing setbacks as temporary hurdles and seeking solutions instead of dwelling on problems. Surround yourself with positive influences and avoid negative energy that could dampen your enthusiasm. A positive attitude can be contagious and foster a supportive and uplifting work environment.

In the insurance industry, resilience is key to weathering the inevitable storms. Understand that setbacks and rejections are part of the process, and they don't define your worth or potential. Develop coping mechanisms to bounce back quickly from disappointments and focus on the lessons learned from each experience. Resilience allows you to maintain your drive and passion for the business, even during challenging times.

Effective communication is at the heart of insurance sales. Develop strong interpersonal skills to build rapport with clients and understand their unique needs. Listen actively and empathetically to gain insights into their concerns and priorities. Articulate complex insurance concepts clearly and concisely, fostering trust and credibility with your clients. Communication is not just about selling but also about creating long-lasting relationships.

In the rapidly evolving insurance landscape, being open to innovation and adaptability is critical. Embrace new technologies, industry trends, and customer preferences. Stay informed about emerging risks and opportunities, and be proactive in offering innovative solutions. The ability to adapt to change and embrace new ideas will keep you ahead of the competition and position you as a valuable resource for your clients.

Unraveling the Decision-Making Process for Life Insurance

Life insurance is a significant financial decision that provides protection and peace of mind for individuals and their loved ones. The process of making a buying decision for life insurance is complex and influenced by various factors. In this chapter, we will explore the key elements that play a role in people's decision-making process when considering life insurance.

The foundation of the decision-making process begins with understanding one's personal needs and financial goals. Individuals must assess their current financial situation, future responsibilities, and long-term objectives. Factors such as age, marital status, number of dependents, outstanding debts, and desired standard of living all come into play. Life insurance buyers must carefully evaluate how much coverage they require and what type of policies align with their specific needs and objectives.

Recognizing one's financial vulnerabilities is a crucial aspect of making a life insurance purchase. Individuals often consider the potential impact of their absence on their family's financial stability. They might contemplate how the loss of their income could affect their dependents' ability to maintain their current lifestyle, pay for education, or handle outstanding debts. The desire to protect loved ones from financial hardships can be a powerful motivator in the decision-making process.

Life insurance comes in various forms, such as term life, whole life, universal life, and variable life insurance. Each type offers different features, benefits, and premium structures. Buyers must carefully evaluate and compare these options to determine which one best suits their needs. Term life insurance, for example, might be preferred by those seeking affordable coverage for a specific period, while whole life insurance appeals to individuals looking for lifelong protection with potential cash value growth.

Choosing a life insurance policy involves entrusting financial security to an insurance provider. Trust and credibility play a significant role in the decision-making process. Buyers are more likely to choose reputable insurance companies with a track record of prompt claims settlement and excellent customer service. Positive reviews, ratings, and recommendations from friends or family members can enhance an insurer's trustworthiness.

The cost of premiums is a critical consideration for many potential life insurance buyers. Affordability is a significant factor, especially for younger individuals or families on tight budgets. Insurance seekers must evaluate the premium payments against their overall financial commitments and ensure they can comfortably sustain the policy over the long term.

Making an informed decision often requires seeking guidance from insurance professionals. Life insurance agents or financial advisors can help individuals navigate the complexities of various policies, explain the pros and cons of each option, and tailor coverage to meet specific needs. Trustworthy advisors build rapport and earn clients' confidence by offering transparent, unbiased advice.

Emotions also play a role in the decision-making process for life insurance. The thought of leaving loved ones financially secure in the event of an untimely demise can provide a sense of peace and comfort. This emotional aspect can be a powerful driving force behind the decision to purchase life insurance.

Mastering the Art of Selling Permanent Life Insurance as a Tax-Free Retirement Option

Permanent life insurance presents a powerful opportunity for individuals to secure their financial future while enjoying tax-free benefits during retirement. As an insurance professional, understanding how to effectively sell permanent life insurance as a tax-free retirement option can be a game-changer for your clients. In this chapter, we will delve into the strategies and key considerations to successfully market permanent life insurance for tax-free retirement planning.

To sell permanent life insurance as a tax-free retirement option, it is crucial to have a deep understanding of various permanent life insurance policies, including whole life and universal life insurance. Stay up-to-date with the latest industry trends, tax regulations, and policy features to position yourself as a knowledgeable and trustworthy advisor.

Not every client may be suitable for permanent life insurance as a tax-free retirement option. Identify prospects who have long-term financial goals, a need for life insurance protection, and a desire for tax-efficient retirement income. Look for clients who are willing to invest in a policy over an extended period to maximize its benefits fully.

Perform a thorough financial analysis for each client to tailor permanent life insurance solutions to their specific needs.

Understand their current financial situation, retirement goals, income sources, and existing retirement savings plans. Assess potential tax liabilities and demonstrate how a tax-free retirement option can complement their overall financial strategy.

One of the primary selling points of permanent life insurance is its ability to accumulate cash value tax-free. Emphasize the power of tax-free growth, where the policy's cash value increases over time without incurring taxable income. Additionally, illustrate how clients can access the cash value during retirement without facing tax consequences, providing them with a tax-efficient income stream.

Policy loans are a valuable feature of permanent life insurance policies that allow clients to borrow against their cash value without triggering a taxable event. Emphasize the advantages of policy loans, such as flexibility, competitive interest rates, and the potential to maintain a tax-free retirement income stream.

While permanent life insurance offers remarkable tax advantages, it is essential to address potential risks and the importance of maintaining the policy long-term. Discuss the significance of consistent premium payments to build and sustain the cash value and death benefit. Educate clients on the risks associated with policy lapses and how it may impact their retirement strategy.

Present a comprehensive comparison of permanent life insurance as a tax-free retirement option versus other common retirement vehicles, such as traditional IRAs or 401(k)s. Demonstrate how the tax-free growth and withdrawal potential of permanent life insurance can make it a valuable addition to a diversified retirement portfolio.

Every client's financial situation is unique, so avoid adopting a one-size-fits-all approach. Customize permanent life insurance solutions that align with their individual goals, risk tolerance, and retirement vision. Tailor the policy to meet their specific needs and demonstrate the long-term benefits it can offer.

Selling permanent life insurance as a tax-free retirement option requires expertise, empathy, and a deep understanding of your client's financial objectives. By educating yourself about different permanent life insurance policies, identifying ideal prospects, conducting comprehensive financial assessments, and emphasizing tax-free growth and withdrawals, you can position yourself as a trusted advisor. Addressing risk management, highlighting policy loans, and providing comparative analyses will empower your clients to make informed decisions about their tax-efficient retirement planning. Ultimately, mastering the art of selling permanent life insurance as a tax-free retirement option can lead to long-lasting client relationships and financial security for your clients.

Building Strategic Partnerships to Generate Quality Leads

For insurance agents, developing strategic partnerships can be a game-changer when it comes to generating high-quality leads. By collaborating with complementary businesses and professionals, insurance agents can access a broader pool of potential clients and establish a reputation as a trusted advisor. In this chapter, we will explore the steps and best practices to set up strategic partnerships that foster lead generation and business growth.

The first step in building strategic partnerships is to identify businesses and professionals whose services align with your target market. Look for partners in related industries, such as real estate agents, mortgage brokers, financial advisors, accountants, and estate planning attorneys. Seek out individuals and organizations that serve a similar client base but offer different products or services, creating a win-win situation for both parties.

Research Potential Partners

Once you have a list of potential partners, conduct thorough research to understand their business practices, reputation, and clientele. Consider their track record, values, and customer reviews. Look for partners who share your commitment to professionalism, ethics, and exceptional customer service. A successful strategic partnership depends on mutual trust and respect.

Establish a Value Proposition

Before approaching potential partners, articulate a clear value proposition that outlines the benefits of collaborating with your insurance agency. Explain how a partnership can enhance value to clients by offering comprehensive insurance solutions. Emphasize the advantages of referring clients to your agency, such as personalized service, competitive products, and reliable claims handling.

Initiate the Conversation

Reach out to potential partners to initiate the conversation about collaboration. Be professional, respectful, and transparent about your intentions. Offer to meet in person or arrange a virtual meeting to discuss the mutual benefits of a strategic partnership. Focus on how the partnership can create a symbiotic relationship where both parties can grow their businesses through increased referrals.

Create a Referral Program

Develop a structured referral program that incentivizes your strategic partners to refer clients to your insurance agency. This program should be easy to understand and implement. Consider offering referral fees, exclusive promotions, or reciprocal referrals to encourage active participation from your partners.

Nurture the Relationship

Building successful strategic partnerships requires ongoing effort and communication. Stay in touch with your partners regularly, share updates on insurance products or industry insights, and celebrate successes together. Attend networking events, conferences, and social gatherings where you can strengthen the relationship further. Demonstrating your commitment to the partnership fosters trust and strengthens the bond.

Provide Excellent Service to Referred Clients

When a strategic partner refers a client to your agency, ensure you provide exceptional service from the first interaction. Tailor your approach to meet the client's needs, provide personalized insurance solutions, and demonstrate genuine care for their well-being. Delivering excellent service to referred clients not only fosters trust but also encourages repeat business and more referrals in the future.

Measure and Review the Partnership's Impact

Regularly assess the effectiveness of your strategic partnerships in generating leads and business growth. Track the number of referrals received, conversion rates, and the overall impact on your agency's bottom line. Analyze which partnerships are most fruitful and consider refining your approach or expanding to new collaborations based on these insights.

How Insurance Agents Can Differentiate from the Competition

In today's competitive insurance landscape, standing out from the crowd is essential for insurance agents to attract and retain clients. Differentiating yourself from the competition requires a thoughtful approach that highlights your unique value proposition and builds lasting relationships with customers. In this chapter, we will explore various strategies and tactics that insurance agents can employ to set themselves apart and gain a competitive edge.

Understanding your strengths and areas of expertise is crucial in defining your niche. Identify a specific target market or industry segment where you can excel and provide exceptional service. Focusing on a niche allows you to become a specialist in that area, making you a go-to resource for clients with specific insurance needs.

Providing personalized service is a powerful way to differentiate yourself from larger insurance companies. Take the time to get to know your clients, understand their unique needs, and tailor insurance solutions accordingly. By showing genuine care and attention to each client, you can build strong relationships and foster trust.

Go beyond basic insurance offerings and provide comprehensive solutions that address various aspects of your clients' lives and businesses. Offer risk management assessments, customized policies, and bundled coverage options that meet your clients' evolving needs.

Position yourself as an industry expert by staying up-to-date with the latest insurance trends, regulations, and innovations. Share your knowledge through informative blog posts, articles, and social media content. Demonstrating expertise builds credibility and reinforces your clients' confidence in your abilities.

Efficient and empathetic claims handling can significantly impact clients' perception of your services. Streamline the claims process, offer guidance, and be proactive in resolving issues promptly. Clients who experience a smooth claims process are more likely to become loyal advocates for your agency.

Leverage technology to enhance the client experience and streamline administrative tasks. Invest in customer relationship management (CRM) software, online quoting tools, and mobile applications to offer convenience and efficiency to your clients.

Be transparent with your pricing and provide clients with clear explanations of premium structures and coverage details. Avoid hidden fees or surprises that could erode trust. Transparency builds credibility and fosters long-term relationships with clients.

Create a professional website that showcases your expertise and services. Utilize social media platforms to engage with potential clients and share valuable content. An active online presence allows you to reach a broader audience and expand your client base.

Educate your clients on insurance-related topics and risk management strategies. Host webinars, workshops, or seminars that provide valuable insights and solutions to common insurance challenges. Becoming a source of knowledge positions you as a trusted advisor.

Ask satisfied clients for testimonials and reviews that highlight their positive experiences with your agency. Display these testimonials on your website and marketing materials to build social proof and instill confidence in potential clients.

Setting yourself apart from the competition requires a proactive and client-centric approach. By identifying your niche, emphasizing personalized service, offering comprehensive solutions, and showcasing your expertise, you can differentiate yourself as a top insurance agent. Utilizing technology, providing transparent pricing, and cultivating a strong online presence further strengthens your position in the market. By consistently delivering exceptional service and fostering lasting relationships, you can build a loyal client base and thrive in the competitive insurance industry.

Conclusion

Everybody has heard about the significance of your Mind, Body, and Spirit working together in harmony. The three work together to shape your life and your beliefs. More importantly, it shapes your ability to succeed.

Succeed in what? You may be asking yourself. When it comes to your entire life as a whole, if you are not in harmony with all three of these areas, you can feel overwhelmed, scared, impatient, and unknowing about any situation or situations in your life. And if the situation doesn't turn out like you thought that it would. Well, then, you feel like a failure.

So how does this relate to sales? If you are not happy at home, struggling with closing the sale. And if you see everyone else at the top except you. This will affect your mojo.

Just because you may be having a hard time in sales doesn't mean it's your fault. We will look into time-tested techniques that we have covered in this book. They have proven themselves to work. I hope this helped you understand your own subconscious mind. And how to re-program your brain for success.

Read this book again and again. It will inspire you every time you read it. And if you're a novice in the sales world, use this step-by-step guide to unlock your inner potential. And for the expert, uncover more ideas and ways to persuade your clients to make more money than ever before.

www.ingramcontent.com/pod-product-compliance
Lightning Source LLC
Chambersburg PA
CBHW060842260726
48661CB00002B/566